Hannelore Schäl and Ulla Abdalla
Toys Made of Clay

Hannelore Schäl and Ulla Abdalla

Toys Made of Clay

Photos and illustrations by Angela Wiesner

Can I help you?

CHILDRENS PRESS ®
CHICAGO

Library of Congress Cataloging-in-Publication Data

Schäl, Hannelore.
    [Spielsachen aus Ton.   English]
    Toys made of clay / by Hannelore Schäl, Ulla Abdalla, Angela Wiesner.
        p.   cm.
    Translation of: Spielsachen aus Ton.
    Instructions for making a variety of art projects and games out of
clay.
    ISBN 0-516-09256-1
    1. Pottery craft—Juvenile literature.   2. Toy making—Juvenile
literature.   [1. Pottery craft.   2. Handicraft.]   I. Abdalla,
Ulla.   II. Wiesner, Angela.   III. Title.
TT921.S3313   1989
745.592—dc20

89-22253
CIP
AC

Translation by Mrs. Werner Lippmann and Mrs. Ruth Bookey

Published in the United States in 1990 by Childrens Press®, Inc.,
5440 North Cumberland Avenue, Chicago, IL 60656.

Table of Contents

Let's go for a ride in the jungle!

Clay Is a Small Piece of Earth

There are different kinds of clay.

Clay is made from finely ground rocks. Over many millions of years, these rocks have been brought from the mountains into the valleys by wind and water. Today we find various clay deposits, depending on the color of the original rocks. Clay can be red, yellow, gray, black, or white.

Where to Buy Clay

Clay can be bought in pottery stores or in handicraft stores.

 The clay you buy is all ready to use. You can start right in making things with it.

You may find clay in your own yard; clay is almost everywhere. When you find clay, you can try to make some little toys from it and just let the clay dry without having it fired in a kiln.

Wedging

Sometimes the clay has air pockets. Then the clay must be pounded or thrown (wedged) to get these out. Throw the piece of clay firmly against a board or on a tabletop several times.

Can I help you?

How to Cut Off a Piece of Clay

Put a string around the middle of your piece of clay. Cross the ends of the string and pull tightly to cut the clay in half. Put the clay you are not using into a plastic bag and close the bag tightly so that the clay won't dry out.

How to Shape Clay

Only soft clay can be shaped. Clay shrinks a bit and gets hard when it dries. When you are making the marble games, remember to make the paths for the marbles wide enough.

How to Moisten Dried-Out Clay

Add some water to dry or leftover pieces and knead thoroughly.

Too-dry Clay

Make holes in the clay. Fill with water, let stand, then knead.

Hardened Clay

Put into water to soften. Then knead.

Too-wet Clay

Let dry in air for a while, then knead.

Drying Clay Toys

Clay should dry slowly. Cover your clay toys with plastic sheets and let them dry in a cool place. Small clay pieces need one week to dry. Big pieces need two weeks.

Firing

The dried clay pieces can be fired in a kiln. Kilns are available in pottery stores. (CAUTION: Do not try to use a kiln yourself. Have an adult do the firing for you.)

In the Table of Contents, we have marked the pieces that should be fired in a kiln with this kiln sign.

The Best Way to Do It

You will need: A wooden board 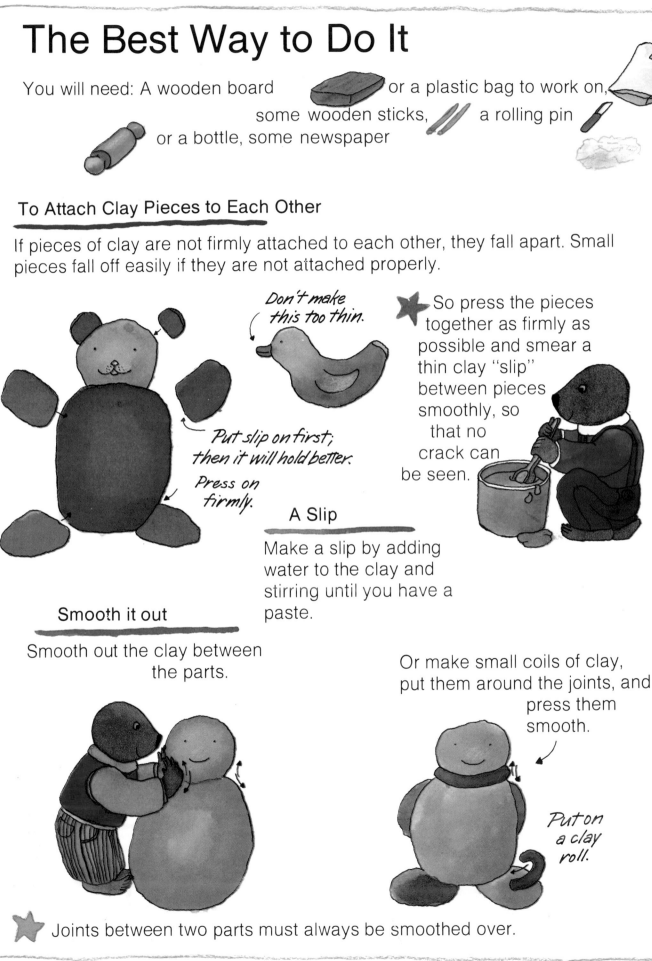 or a plastic bag to work on, some wooden sticks, a rolling pin or a bottle, some newspaper

To Attach Clay Pieces to Each Other

If pieces of clay are not firmly attached to each other, they fall apart. Small pieces fall off easily if they are not attached properly.

Don't make this too thin.

Put slip on first; then it will hold better.

Press on firmly.

⭐ So press the pieces together as firmly as possible and smear a thin clay "slip" between pieces smoothly, so that no crack can be seen.

A Slip

Make a slip by adding water to the clay and stirring until you have a paste.

Smooth it out

Smooth out the clay between the parts.

Or make small coils of clay, put them around the joints, and press them smooth.

Put on a clay roll.

⭐ Joints between two parts must always be smoothed over.

Pieces of clay that are thicker than 1 inch crack in the kiln. Hollow out thicker pieces, or make holes underneath the piece with a small stick or a knitting needle.

To Hollow Out Clay

Use your fingers or a spoon to dig out clumps of clay. Make sure the walls of your dish are of equal thickness (½ to 1 inch) when you finish hollowing out.

If you take too much clay from the sides when you are hollowing out, just smear fresh clay on the area as you need it.

To Roll Out Clay

Press the lump of clay flat, then roll it with a rolling pin or a bottle, keeping the thickness as even as possible.

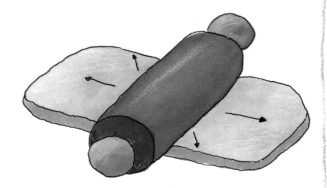

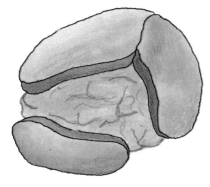

To Make a Hollow Clay Ball

Flatten a lump of clay with your fist. Make two of these and wrap them around a crumpled ball of newspaper. Blend the clay well between pieces. Continue to put flat pieces of clay over the paper ball until it is completely covered.

When to Paint Clay

After your clay figures have completely dried and/or have been fired, they are ready to be painted.

Painting tip: Use a lacquer (or shellac) over your colors, or use lacquer paint. The finish will be glossy and waterproof.

A Well

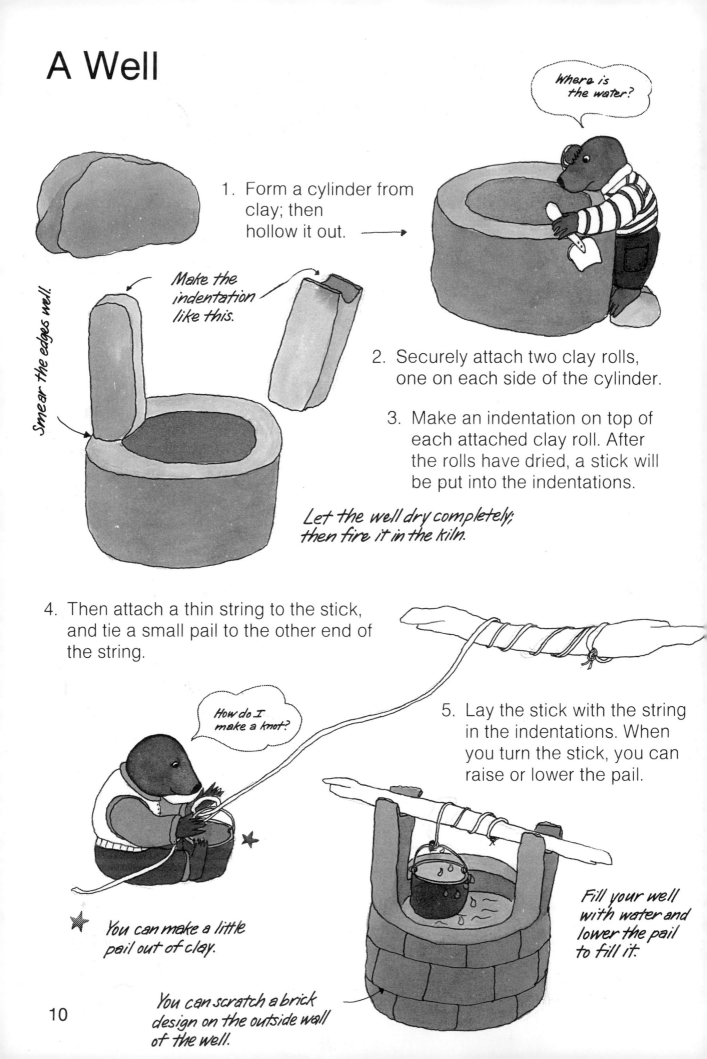

Where is the water?

1. Form a cylinder from clay; then hollow it out. →

Make the indentation like this.

Smear the edges well.

2. Securely attach two clay rolls, one on each side of the cylinder.

3. Make an indentation on top of each attached clay roll. After the rolls have dried, a stick will be put into the indentations.

Let the well dry completely; then fire it in the kiln.

4. Then attach a thin string to the stick, and tie a small pail to the other end of the string.

How do I make a knot?

5. Lay the stick with the string in the indentations. When you turn the stick, you can raise or lower the pail.

★ You can make a little pail out of clay.

Fill your well with water and lower the pail to fill it.

You can scratch a brick design on the outside wall of the well.

A Little Treasure Box

1. Make a clay slab about 2 inches thick.

2. Cut the slab into two pieces with a string. Put string around the slab, cross the ends in front, and pull the ends firmly. The string will cut the slab into two pieces.

3. Carefully hollow out both halves.

4. Inside one half put a secret letter or some other treasure that you don't want anyone to see.

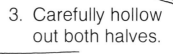

5. Put the other half on top and close the crack with soft clay. Then let the whole thing dry.

Open the treasure box in this way.

Scratch a groove where the halves meet and then tap the groove gently with a hammer.

Finger Puppets

Make a little tiger.

1. Spread your fingers a bit and press them into a slab of clay. Deepen the finger impressions a little more, since the clay will shrink when it dries.

2. Use a lump of clay for the head. Make two ears with your fingers. Scratch in a face. Fasten legs under the body. Smear all the joints well.

Stop!

Don't forget the tail!

Make finger puppets.

2. When making the face, form a nose, ears, and hair or a hat separately and press them into the head.

3. Paint or shellac the animals when they are completely dry.

1. Make a clay ball and press a hole into it with your finger.

An Erupting Volcano

You will need: Clay, a bowl about 4½ inches deep, an empty vegetable can about 4½ inches high and 3 inches in diameter, aluminum foil, baking soda, white vinegar, red or yellow food coloring, newspaper

1. Put foil over the inverted bowl.

2. Press many small clay lumps on the bowl, starting at the bottom.

3. Leave an opening 3 inches in diameter at the top.

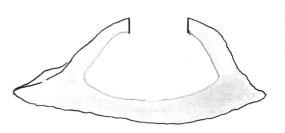

smear every lump with slip.

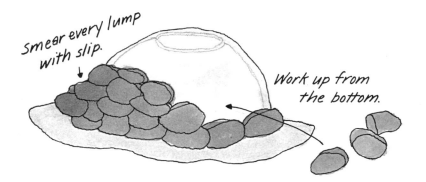

Work up from the bottom.

4. Remove the bowl, let the volcano dry, and have it fired in the kiln.

5. Put 1/3 cup of baking soda in the can.

6. Place the volcano over the can so that the opening in the top fits over the rim of the can. Seal the joint between the can and the volcano with clay. There must be a tight seal. Build up a clay crater over the rim, leaving a hole in the top for the eruption. Let it all dry. (Do not put the volcano with the can into the kiln.)

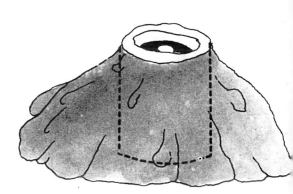

To make the volcano erupt:
Put several thicknesses of newspaper under the volcano. Put a few drops of food coloring into 1 cup of vinegar to color it red or yellow. Pour the vinegar into the volcano and watch it erupt. You can add more soda and vinegar as needed to make it erupt again.

Snail Game

1. Make a long, thin body out of clay.

2. Coil up a long roll of clay.

3. Shape the coil into a cone to form a snail house. Fill the inside of the cone with mo[re] clay.

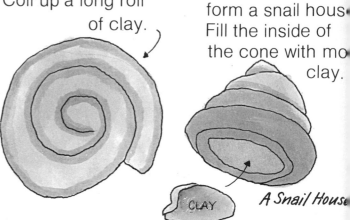

CLAY

A Snail House

4. Set the snail house on top of the snail body.

5. Make a second, larger snail house and leave it hollow inside. Make sure the inside is nice and smooth. It should be able to fit over the smaller snail house.

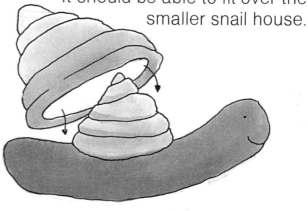

The die

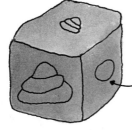

Make one small die out of clay. Scratch the signs shown into it.

The signs mean:

= *Take another turn.*

= *Don't move.*

○ = *Go back one step.*

6. ☆Game Rules ☆
You can draw the board on a large piece of paper. Each perso[n] throws the die and moves his or her snail accordingly. Th[e] snail that wins gets th[e] bigger house to wea[r]

You could draw the game on a sidewalk with chalk.

18

Toy Stove

1. Hollow out a 2½-inch-thick clay block. Make the walls ½ inch thick.

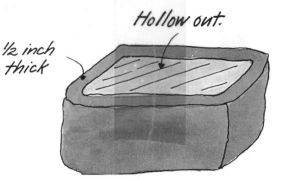

Hollow out.

½ inch thick

Turn the hollowed block over.

2. Turn your stove over. With a pointed stick, scratch in a door, a burner, and a warming plate. Also put in a brick pattern around the walls.

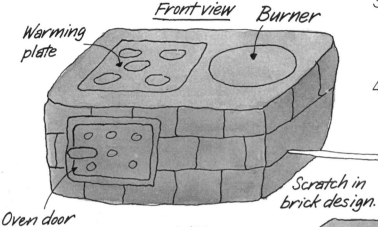

Front view *Burner*

Warming plate

Oven door

Scratch in brick design.

3. Make some holes in the warming plate and the oven door.

4. Cut out the burner hole. In the back of your stove, cut out a door. Later you can put a small flashlight through this opening to be the stove's fire.

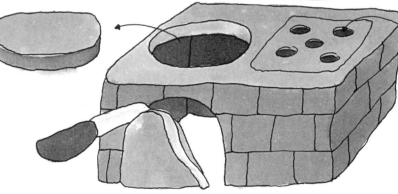

Back view

Make holes in warming plate.

5. Let the stove dry; then have it fired in the kiln.

You can make some cooking pots, too!

Marble Game

1. Flatten some clay into a circle about 1 inch thick.

1 inch thick

2. Starting from the center, hollow out a path for marbles. Make sure the path is wider than a marble, because the clay will shrink when it dries.

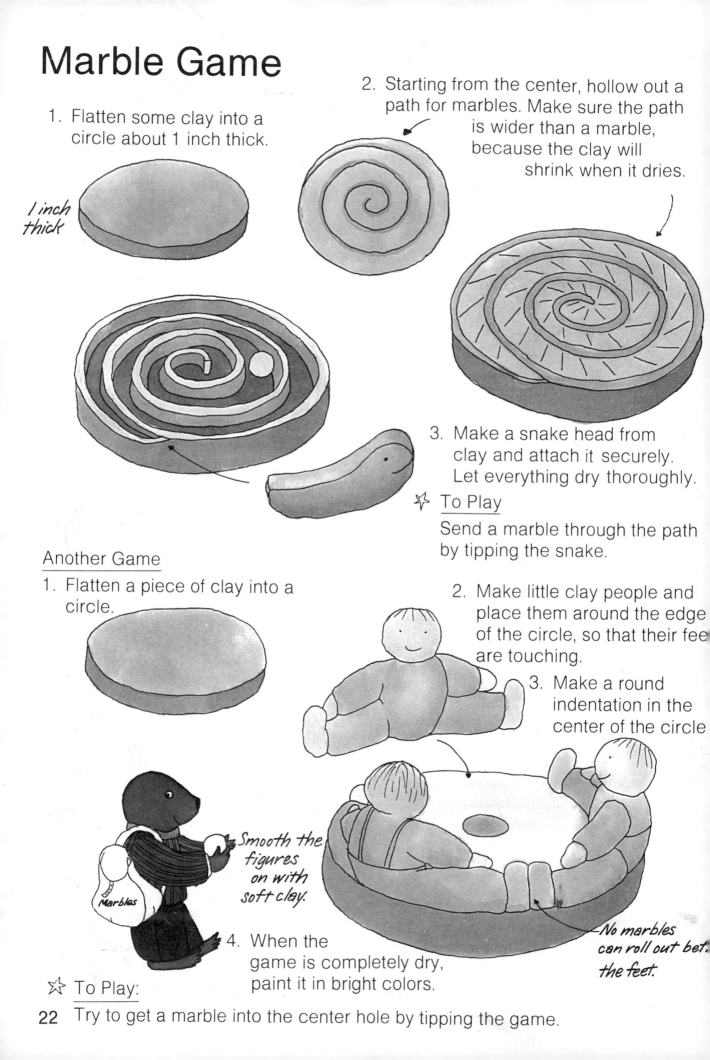

3. Make a snake head from clay and attach it securely. Let everything dry thoroughly.

☆ To Play

Send a marble through the path by tipping the snake.

Another Game

1. Flatten a piece of clay into a circle.

2. Make little clay people and place them around the edge of the circle, so that their feet are touching.

3. Make a round indentation in the center of the circle

Smooth the figures on with soft clay.

Marbles

4. When the game is completely dry, paint it in bright colors.

No marbles can roll out bet. the feet.

☆ To Play:

Try to get a marble into the center hole by tipping the game.

Paper-Ball Shooter

1. Use a thick felt-tip marker to poke a hole ⟶ in a clay ball.

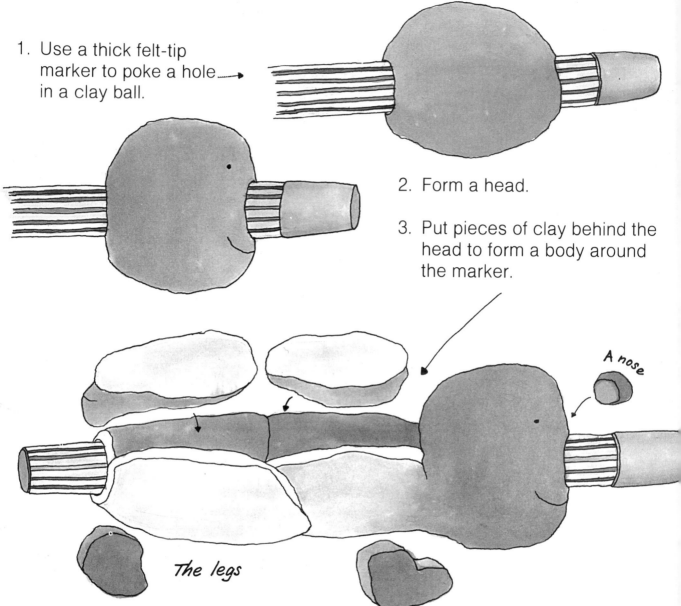

2. Form a head.

3. Put pieces of clay behind the head to form a body around the marker.

A nose

The legs

4. Smooth out the clay between the head and the body. Also make arms, legs, and a nose. Make everything nice and smooth.

5. Remove the felt-tip marker. (Turn it while you are pulling it out, and it will come out more easily.)

6. Let the shooter dry and then have it fired in the kiln. Paint it later.

★ How to use the shooter ✦☆
Form very small balls out of paper and blow them through the clay tube. Who can blow the farthest?

Dancing Toys

1. Make a clay ball as large as a tennis ball.

2. Poke a deep hole in the ball with your finger.

3. Stick a piece of elastic (about 20 inches long) into the hole as shown.

Double the elastic band.

Clay

4. Now close the opening by stuffing more clay into the hole. Make sure it is good and tight. Both ends of the elastic should hang out.

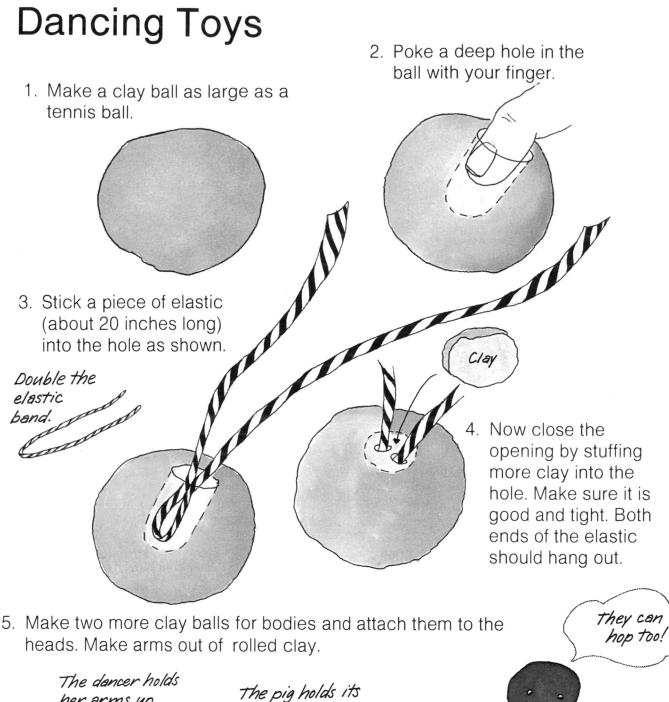

5. Make two more clay balls for bodies and attach them to the heads. Make arms out of rolled clay.

The dancer holds her arms up.

The pig holds its arms close to its body.

Make the surface very smooth.

They can hop too!

6. When the figures are dry, you can paint them.

Twist the elastic and then let it go as you hold it at the top. You'll be amazed at how long your figures "dance."

A Calendar

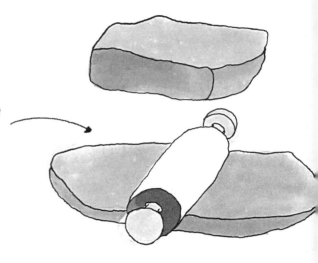

1. Cut a thick slice of clay.

2. With a rolling pin or a bottle, roll the slice into a slab about 1 inch thick.

3. With a sharp stick, draw a calendar on the slab, as shown in the picture at the right.

4. With a larger stick, poke holes beside the days, months, and dates. Later you can put short sticks into the holes to tell what day and date it is.

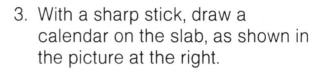

My calendar's heavy. I'll need a big nail to hang it up.

5. Smooth out the edges of your calendar. Then make two big holes at the top, so that you can hang it up later. Make sure the holes go all the way through.

6. Cover the calendar loosely with plastic wrap and let it dry for two weeks. Then you can have it fired in the kiln.

Let it dry for 2 weeks under plastic wrap.

28

A Circus

1. Make a clown from a thick roll of clay.

Make a pointed head.

Draw a face with a stick.

2. Make another clay roll and press it flat in the middle. Set the clown on the flat part.

Make sure it's secure by smearing extra clay where two pieces join.

3. Bend the ends of the roll toward the clown's body so that they look like arms.

4. Move the clown back and forth until it rocks smoothly.

A Top

Make a clay ball. Form a cone from the ball. Make a handle. Let it dry before you play with it.

Turn it here!

Clown Headstand

1. Make a flat clay slab. Cut through on both ends and bend apart slightly, as the drawing shows.

2. Press a small clay ball into one end. Let the figure dry.

3. Position the clown on his head and one arm, and he'll stand by himself.

Paint your clown in bright colors.

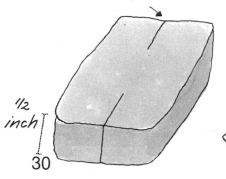

½ inch

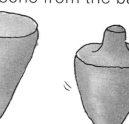

Horse and Wagon

1. Bend down the ends of a thick clay roll.

2. Stick on another piece of clay and shape a horse's head.

Press the head on and secure it by smoothing on extra clay.

3. Shape the horse's body.

Leave the front and back legs as one piece.

4. To make the wagon:

   Hollow out a big piece of clay. Poke two sticks through the wagon walls. Make a hole in the front end. Later you'll put a string through this hole.

5. The wheels are made from a clay roll.

Make a hole.

The string

6. Let the wheels dry before you mount them on the wagon. When you put them on, secure them with pieces of cork on the outside.

Put a cork outside each wheel.

   Let everything dry thoroughly.

Watercress Garden

1. Use a square of clay 1½ inches thick for your garden.

2. Pressing with your fingers, make a ditch along the edges for water.

The rim shouldn't be thicker than 1½ inches.

The ditch

3. With your hands, make furrows in the field. Press the furrows up a little in the middle.

4. Let the garden dry thoroughly and then have it fired in the kiln.

5. Sow the watercress seeds.

Make a little house for your garden.

Put the house on the edge. Make it secure by smearing on soft clay.

WATERCRESS

6. In a few days t watercress ca be harvested.

Don't forget wate

Let's move into the watercress field.

Rocking Duck

1. Bend up the sides of a thick clay roll.

2. Hollow out the body in the middle of the roll, pressing the clay to both sides.

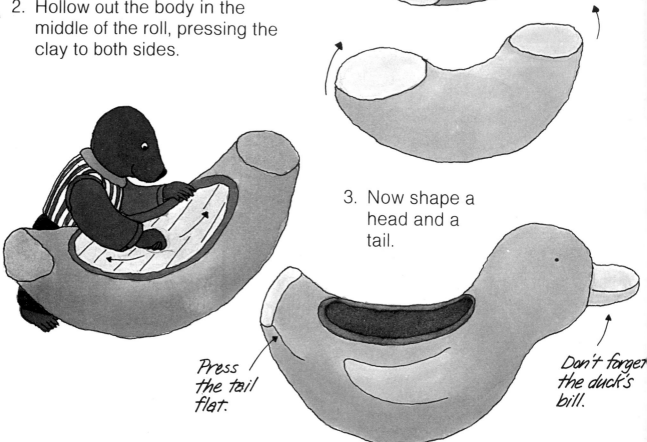

3. Now shape a head and a tail.

Press the tail flat.

Don't forget the duck's bill.

4. Rock the duck back and forth on a flat surface until it can rock by itself.

5. Let the duck dry completely. Then paint and shellac it.

Castle With a Moat

1. Cut a big piece of clay about 5 inches high.

2. With your fist, pound the clay into a wide, round shape like a bowl, about 3½ inches high.

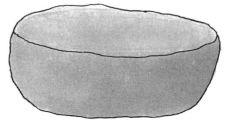

3. Hollow out the bowl shape. The edge should be about 1 inch thick.

4. Put a ball of crushed paper underneath the bowl. Now there's a little hill in the middle.

Paper ball

5. Make a little castle out of clay and put it on top of the hill. Build a bridge over the moat on one side.

The castle will sit on the hill.

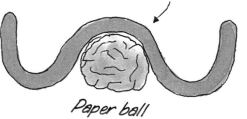

The castle's flag

6. The castle and moat must dry completely before you have it fired in the kiln.

☆ In the meantime you can make little boats and a flag for the castle. (See the drawings.)

A man in the castle

A boat made from a piece of bark

A boat made from a nutshell

A Rattle and a Musical Canoe

The Rattle

1. Make a ball of crumpled paper. Press pieces of clay all around it. Press them good and tight. Leave an opening in the ball.

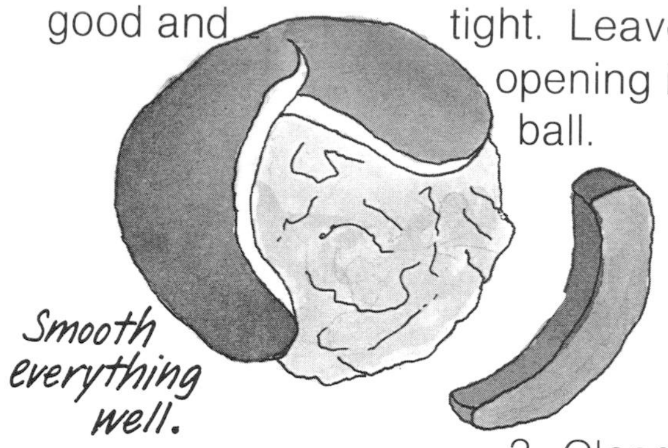

Smooth everything well.

2. Pull the paper out through the hole. Fill the ball with tiny dried clay balls.

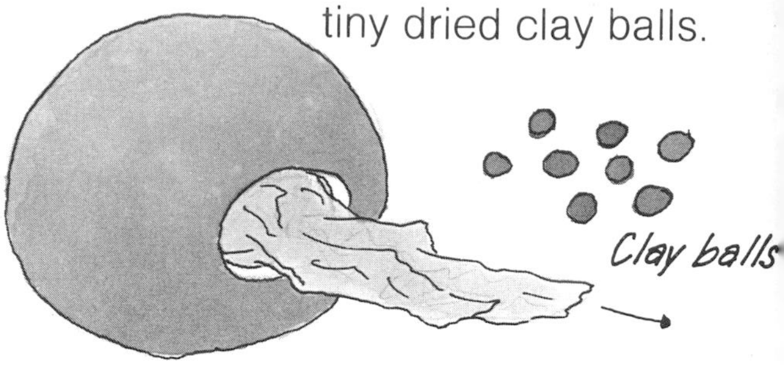

Clay balls

3. Close the hole with clay. Make a handle and put it in on. Smooth the seams.

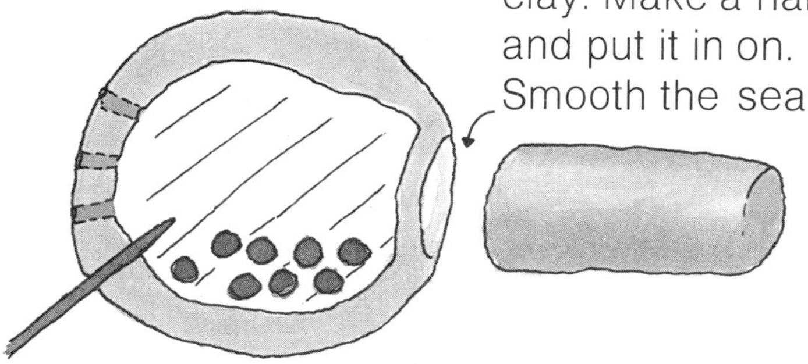

Shake the rattle like this.

4. Poke little holes in the rattle and let it dry thoroughly Paint the rattle a bright color!

Musical Canoe

1. Form a canoe shape and hollow it out.

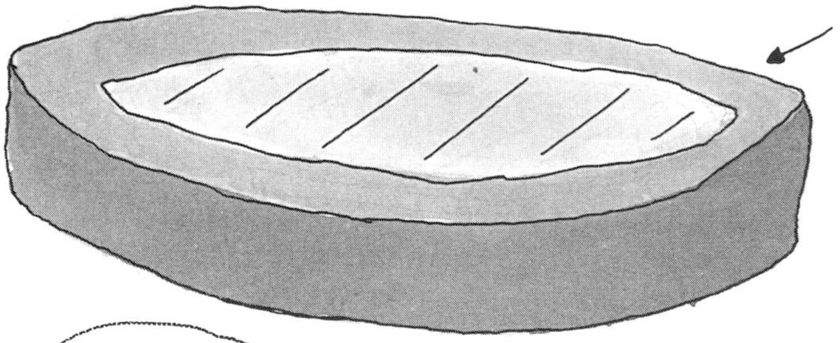

2. Poke holes in the sides.

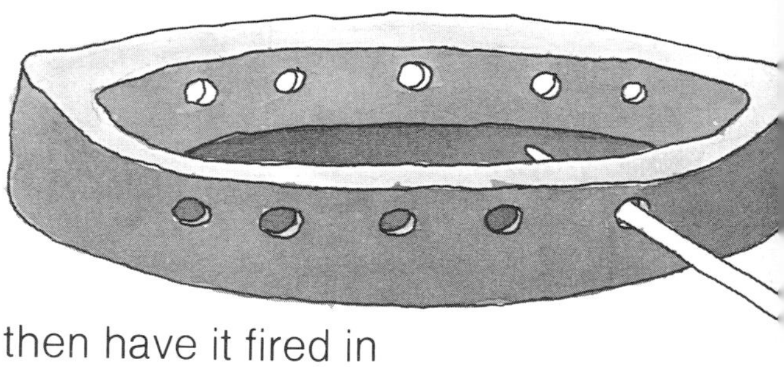

3. Let it dry and then have it fired in the kiln.
4. Paint the boat.

5. Pull a rubber band through the holes, as shown in the diagram. Fasten with knots. When you pluck the rubber band, you'll hear music.

This is an Indian pattern.

Viking Village

1. To make the Vikings:
   Form a pointed cone out of a clay ball.

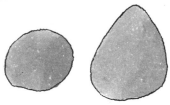

   Eric and Brunhilde

2. Make some hair out of clay and stick it with slip to the top of the cone. Make a face with a pointed stick.

   Hair

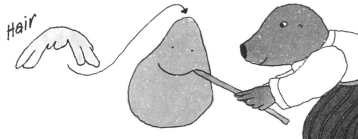

3. When the Vikings are dry, you can paint some clothes on them.

4. The windmill is made just like the fragrance ball on page 50. Cut out windows and doors with a knife. (CAUTION: Be careful when using a knife, or have an adult do the cutting for you.)

The roof

Make the roof from a thin slice of clay, and stick it to the ball with a clay slip.

☆ Insert a little stick into one side of the mill to hold the "blade." Let everything dry.

5. Shape your windmill "blade." Put a hole in the middle. Let it dry. Then put the blade on the stick in the windmill. It will really turn!

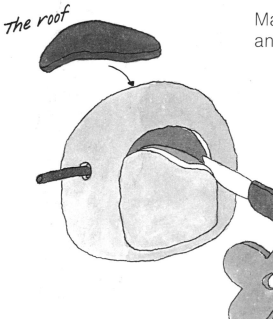

The windmill blade

☆☆ Make some animals for the Vikings. Make an indentation in the back of an animal so that a Viking can fit into it and go for a ride.

A rider

42

Potato Oven

1. Form a thick clay block.

2. Hollow out one side, pushing the dug-out clay toward the front, to make the front plate bigger and stronger.

Front plate

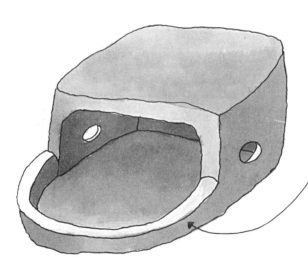

3. Shape a rim around the front plate. Poke a hole on each side, as in the drawing.

Smooth it well.

4. Put small pieces of clay all around the top edge of the oven. Smooth them all together into a rim. The top of the oven should be very smooth.

5. When the clay is good and dry, it can be fired in the kiln.

6. The fire can be made with small pieces of charcoal. (CAUTION: Do not use the oven by yourself. Ask an adult to help you. Do not make a charcoal fire indoors.)

Cooking tips: Slice potatoes, spread them with oil, and put them in rows on top of the stove to roast.

Elephant

1. Form a big elephant out of clay.

2. Shape a head at one end.

3. Make some ears and a trunk. Attach them securely by smoothing on extra clay where they join the head.

If you bend the trunk, the elephant can carry little sticks.

The ears

The tail

4. Hollow out the body at the bottom so that you can attach four legs.

Hollow out

5. Set in the thick legs.

Have patience. The elephant must be good and dry before you can play with it. You may have the elephant fired in the kiln if you wish.

Let's go for a ride in the jungle!

Above and Below the Ground

1. Shape a thick slab of clay and make two holes in it for hanging.

Front   Back

Holes in the back

2. Dig out some tunnels and hiding places for the earth creatures.

3. Make some earthworms, mice, and snails out of clay.

The earth creatures

4. What grows under the ground? Make some vegetables and set them into the ground. Let the leaves stick out at the top.

And where is _my_ nest?

Let everything dry and then fire it in the kiln.

☆ What's happening? ☆

The little mice are nestling in their den.
The earthworm is watching for rain. The snail is eating carrot leaves.

48

49

Fragrance Ball

1. Crumple some newspapers into a ball.

2. Take pieces of clay and flatten them out on a table. Wrap the pieces around the paper ball until it is all covered.

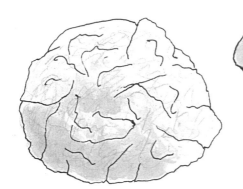

Make everything smooth and seamless.

3. Let the clay dry partially.

4. Make two holes on one side of the ball. Later you will pull a ribbon through these holes to hang the ball. Use a little stick to poke some air holes in the upper part of the ball.

Pull a ribbon through the holes.

5. Make another hole in the bottom of the ball, and pull out the paper.

6. Scratch some designs in the ball.

7. When the ball is completely dry, paint it with poster paint and shellac it.

8. What smells do you like? Pine needles? Rose petals? Spices? Fill the ball with your favorite fragrant things.

Close the opening on the bottom with tape.

A Small Garden

1. For your garden you need a large, thick slab of clay.

2. Dig out several hollow places. All walls and the bottom should be about 2 inches thick. (See the drawings.)

Maybe like this →

3. Now let the garden dry for two weeks. Then have it fired in the kiln.

4. Now the garden can be planted. Divide your garden between soil and water. A little meadow with wildflowers would look pretty.

I'll fill this part with water.

Animal Water-Squirters

1. Crumple newspaper into a long shape.

2. Make several flat clay pieces. Cover the paper shape with them. Smooth out all seams.

smooth out well.

3. You can make a fish or a dragon. Shape a head and a mouth. Make a hole in the tip of the snout (this is where the water will come out). Shape the back side of your animal like the paper-ball shooter on page 24.

The hole must go all the way through to the inside.

4. Put a clay pipe on the hole in front.

The dragon needs wings.

5. Let everything dry before you have it fired in the kiln. The paper inside will burn up in the kiln.

6. Hold the front hole closed with your finger and fill your squirter with water from the back. Now blow!

Marble Maiden

1. Form a thick cube of clay so it stands solidly.

2. Shape it into a rounded cone. Use a pencil to poke holes at the bottom so the air can escape.

3. Shape a neck, a head, and a face. Attach some hair.

4. Wrap a roll of clay around the figure. Hollow out the roll so that a marble can roll down the path.

Press firmly and fill in the cracks.

5. Use your fingers to make the path smooth and wide enough for the marbles.

6. Pull up the sides of the marble path a little so that the marble will stay in the path.

Let the marble maiden dry. Then paint it.

7. To make a game board:
Make a flat, round disk of clay. Press in marbles to make holes. When the holes are dry, mark them with numbers.

Like this

★ Rules of the game:
Each player gets five marbles and in turn lets one marble roll down the path on the marble maiden onto the game board. The number of the hole that marble lands on is the score for that turn. The player with the most points is the winner.

☆ *Who has the most points?*

Stone on Stone

1. Cut bricks out of clay, about ½ inch high.

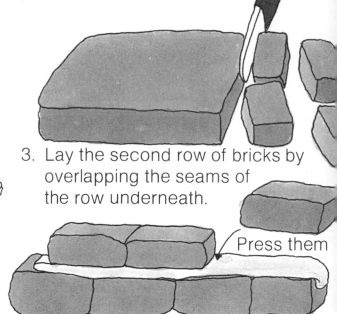

2. To build a wall:
   Make a row of bricks. Cover the top of the row with a clay slip.

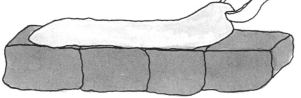

3. Lay the second row of bricks by overlapping the seams of the row underneath.

   Press them

Repeat the pattern row by row.

4. To make a window:
   Leave an opening as you build the wall. When the wall is high enough, lay a longer "brick" across the top.

5. Continue building. Make the wall as high as you wish.

6. The roof:
   Build the roof out of small sticks. You can cover it with moss, grass or small clay shingles.

Tie the sticks together with string as shown.

7. You can also make your wall out of stones made from clay balls.

Slip

This is easy!

Use slip between the rows as you did with the bricks. You could make some clay people as well.

Slip

58

Hot-Dog Grill

1. Cut out a round piece of clay 6 inches in diameter and ½ inch thick.

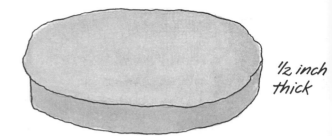

½ inch thick

6 inches in diameter

These will hold the skewers.

2. Attach two thick clay rolls. So that they will be secure, press a clay coil around the base of each one. Smooth out thoroughly.

3. Form each roll into a V shape at the top to hold the skewers.

4. Stick flat pieces of clay around the rim of your grill. This will keep ashes from falling out of the grill.

Tree trunks

5. Scratch a bark pattern into the spit holders. Then they will look like tree trunks.

Grilled vegetables are also tasty.

6. Let the grill dry thoroughly, then have it fired in the kiln.

Take the grill outdoors. Put little hot dogs on a skewer. Ask an adult to grill them over some charcoal.

Bear Cave

1. Prepare a large clump of clay by wedging, until it has the desired shape for your bear cave.

2. Hollow out the cave. If you take out too much clay, just put some back and smooth it over.

Walls about ½ inch thick

3. Put a chimney on top of the cave and smooth out the joint where it is attached.

4. Cut a window and a door.

I'll get straw and moss for this cave.

Cave animals made of clay

<u>Who will live in the cave?</u>
Gnomes, cave people, or bears?

1. Make a clay body. Make a head, a nose, arms, legs, and feet out of clay and attach them to the body. Press firmly and smooth out.

2. Cut in a face and hair with a stick.

Let everything dry thoroughly.

INDEX